DECEMBER

Ellen Jackson

Illustrated by
Robin DeWitt and Pat DeWitt

Charlesbridge

To Kelly Swanson Turner and Lisa Laird,
with thanks—E. J.

To Gil, Karen, Katie, Kelly,
and Brian DeWitt
—R. D. & P. D.

Did You Know?

December is a month of joy. It is a time of holly and poinsettias, candles and gingerbread.

In the North, the days are crisp and the ground is dusted with fresh snow. The long, cold nights are filled with the aroma of wood smoke. When the temperature falls, birds fluff out their feathers to stay warm.

Evergreen trees, such as fir and spruce, are symbols of this time of year. People once believed that evergreen trees and plants had special powers because they stayed green throughout the winter.

In the Northern Hemisphere, December has fewer daylight hours than any other month. Children get ready for school in the dark, and the sun sets in the late afternoon. People bundle up in coats, scarves, and hats to face the cold.

December's weather can be dreary, but it can also be magical. In his poem "Beautiful Snow" the American poet John Whitaker Watson wrote "Oh! the snow, the beautiful snow, / Filling the sky and the earth below."

Fire has always been an important December symbol. The coming of the cold weather was frightening to some ancient peoples. The Celts would bless a Yule log and keep it burning for twelve days to symbolize the return of warmer, sunnier days. Even today, a burning flame is a sign of hope.

As the holidays and the end of the year approach, many people write notes to their friends and relatives. December is a good month to bake cookies or decorate the house.

Mistletoe, a symbol of peace and friendship, is often placed over doorways in December. In ancient Rome and Britain, enemies who met under the mistletoe would lay down their arms and declare peace for the day. Today people who stand under mistletoe are supposed to get a kiss.

Many winter sports begin in December. When
ponds and lakes freeze solid, people strap on
skates and go gliding across the ice. Whether you
are skating outdoors or on an indoor rink, skates
add wings to your feet!

People have been skating for thousands of years.
Ancient skates made of horse, deer, and elk bone
have been found in many places in Europe.
A five-thousand-year-old pair of
skates, the oldest known, was
found at the bottom of a lake
in Switzerland.

Basketball is a popular winter sport that can be played in a gym even when a snowstorm rages outside. Basketball was first played in Springfield, Massachusetts, in 1891. In that first game, players scored points by throwing a soccer ball into peach baskets nailed at each end of a gymnasium.

It is exciting to watch a fast-paced game of college or professional basketball, but anyone who can run, jump, or throw a ball can enjoy playing the game, too.

The December Birthstone

The birthstone for December is the turquoise, a gem that ranges in color from sky blue to apple green. Four turquoise bracelets are the oldest pieces of jewelry known. They were found in the tomb of King Djer of Egypt, who ruled five thousand years ago. Turquoise has long been prized by Native Americans in the Southwest, who often use it to make beads, belt buckles, bracelets, rings, and necklaces.

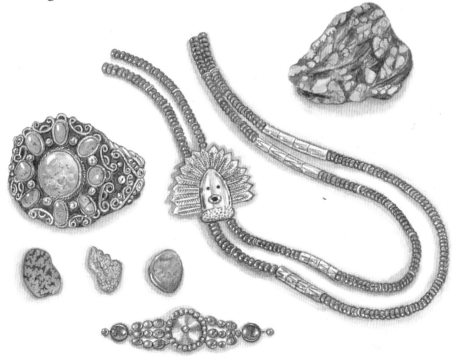

The December Flower

If you were born in December, your special flower is the narcissus. In Greek mythology, Narcissus was a young boy who saw his face reflected in a mountain pool. He was so taken with the beautiful image that he could not tear himself away. Eventually he died and was turned into a narcissus flower.

The December Zodiac

Sagittarius, the archer, is the astrological sign for people with birthdays from November 22 to December 21. People born under this sign are thought to be happy-go-lucky, affectionate, and interested in philosophy and religion. A Sagittarius is always asking questions and is very honest. Sometimes, though, he or she can be a little clumsy.

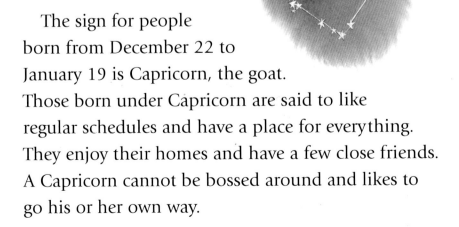

The sign for people born from December 22 to January 19 is Capricorn, the goat. Those born under Capricorn are said to like regular schedules and have a place for everything. They enjoy their homes and have a few close friends. A Capricorn cannot be bossed around and likes to go his or her own way.

The Calendar

December is the twelfth and last month of the year and has thirty-one days. In the early Roman calendar, the year began in March, not January. December was then the tenth month of the year, and its name comes from the Latin word *decem*, which means ten. Originally December had just twenty-nine days. In 46 B.C., Julius Caesar added two days to give it thirty-one days, its present number.

The last day of December is also the last day of the year, a time for fun and celebration. On December 31, people pause at midnight to cheer, sing songs, and say good-bye to the old year before welcoming the new.

Sun, Sky, and Weather

In the woods, the brilliant colors of fall have been replaced by browns and grays. Trees look like skeletons, rattling in the wind.

On the prairie, December weather can range from sunny and mild to freezing cold. Severe snowstorms, or blizzards, sometimes rage across the countryside. Blizzards have winds that reach thirty-five miles per hour or more. After a blizzard, children make caves and tunnels in snowdrifts that can be as high as two-story buildings.

In the Mojave Desert, December days are often warm and mild. Many animals are active in the winter months. It's not unusual to see harvester ants looking for food, or a rattlesnake sunning itself on a rock.

The Anglo-Saxons, who settled in Britain in the fifth and sixth centuries, had two names for December. They called December *Heligh monath*, or holy month, because Christmas comes in December. They also called it *Yule monath* because it was their custom to burn a Yule log at Christmas. The December full moon has been called the long night moon or the cold moon by some Native American peoples of the Northeast.

Animals in December

Some insects take shelter for the winter. Most wasps die in the fall, but the queen wasp may crawl into a crack in a building to wait for spring. Female mosquitoes may cling to a basement wall or cabinet door. Jumping spiders make tiny sleeping bags of silk and fall asleep under stones.

Buntings and nuthatches winter in the Northeast woods. Buntings are white birds that ride the wind like snowflakes. Nuthatches are short and fat with beady black eyes. They can walk down a tree trunk headfirst with their tails pointing to the sky!

In December, bighorn sheep battle one another for mates. Two males rear up on their hind legs and run toward each other, dropping to all fours just before they meet. Their heads collide with a crack, making a sound that can be heard a mile away.

On the prairie, snowshoe rabbits have grown white coats. These rabbits also grow hair between their toes to keep from sinking into the snow. Snowshoe rabbits eat pine needles, bark, and even birds.

If you live in the suburbs of the Southwest, you might see a coyote in the winter. Coyotes sometimes make their dens in old buildings or abandoned cars. When food is scarce, they roam through yards. They will eat almost anything—mice, dog food, garbage, fruits, and vegetables. Many strange items have been found in the stomachs of coyotes, including tin cans and flashlight batteries.

Plants in December

December is the best time to hear the sounds of the woods. When the ground is frozen and the trees are bare, sound waves travel farther. You can hear the creak of tree branches blowing in the wind, the crunch of leaves underfoot, or the boom of ice cracking on a lake.

Some trees have special ways to survive the cold weather. The branches of pine trees are covered with wax-coated needles. This wax seals moisture inside the needles and protects them from the cold, dry wind. The twigs of some oak trees are coated in a velvet fuzz that acts as a windbreak during winter storms.

On the prairie, the first snowstorm beats down the grass. Even though the leaves of some plants have died, their roots are still alive under the snow, and they continue to store nutrients.

In the Sonoran Desert, red fruit dots the stems of the Christmas cholla. The brightly colored fruit helps add a festive note to the bleak desert landscape.

In December, you can buy persimmons in many city supermarkets. The persimmon is a fruit that ripens after the first hard frost. Pudding made from persimmons is a tasty December treat. One superstition says that if the pit of a persimmon is shaped like a knife, winter winds will be biting and cold.

Special Days

Hanukkah

In December, Jews observe the eight days of Hanukkah. This holiday celebrates the successful struggle of a small army of Jews against King Antiochus IV of Syria. After that battle, the Jews returned to Jerusalem to cleanse and rededicate their temple. Upon their return, they found they had only enough oil to light the holy lamps of the temple for just one day. Miraculously, the flames from that oil continued to burn for eight days.

Today during Hanukkah, Jewish families renew their religious faith. They light the eight branches of the menorah, a special candelabra, with a ninth candle called a shamash and recite blessings. Potato pancakes called latkes are served, and children often play games with a spinning top called a dreidel. Songs and gifts are also part of this joyous holiday.

The Winter Solstice

The winter solstice occurs around December 21 and marks the first day of winter in the Northern Hemisphere. On this day, the Northern Hemisphere receives less sunlight, and there are fewer daylight hours than at any other time of the year.

The position of the earth in relation to the sun creates the winter solstice. To see how it works, stick a toothpick in the top of an orange to represent the North Pole. Shine a flashlight, which represents the sun, on the orange, and tilt the North Pole slightly away from the light. Not as much light shines on the top part of the orange. This is the position of the Northern Hemisphere on the winter solstice.

Christmas

For Christians, Christmas is a time of magic and joy. On Christmas Day, December 25, Christians celebrate the birth of Jesus. According to the Bible, a bright star was seen above the manger in Bethlehem where Jesus was born, and an angel announced his birth to shepherds in the fields. Three wise men followed the star to Bethlehem and gave gifts to the baby. This ancient story is retold on December 25 when Christians go to church and give gifts to family and friends.

On Christmas Eve, December 24, many children await the coming of Santa Claus, a jolly figure with a white beard. Santa Claus is said to fly through the air on a magic sleigh, bringing presents and treats. Cards, carols, and Christmas trees add to the fun.

Kwanzaa

Kwanzaa is an African American holiday based on an ancient harvest ceremony. Kwanzaa begins on December 26 and ends on January 1. It is a time for African Americans to honor their ancestors and their African heritage. The name *Kwanzaa* comes from a Swahili phrase that means "first fruits." During this holiday, people decorate their homes in green, red, and black.

On each night of Kwanzaa, African Americans light a candle for one of seven principles—unity, self-determination, collective work, cooperative economics, purpose, creativity, and faith. Taken together, these principles express the spirit and strength of the African American community. On December 31, a feast is held, and there is usually music, dancing, storytelling, and presents.

Famous December Events

On December 20, 1803, President Thomas Jefferson acquired a large piece of land from Napoleon Bonaparte, emperor of France. This sale, known as the Louisiana Purchase, doubled the size of the United States. In 1804, Jefferson sent Meriwether Lewis and William Clark to explore the new territory. Lewis and Clark made maps and described many plants and animals native to the area.

On December 17, 1903, Orville and Wilbur Wright made the first flight in a power-driven, heavier-than-air machine at Kitty Hawk, North Carolina. The flight lasted twelve seconds, and the airplane flew 120 feet. Orville and Wilbur had experimented for three years with kites and gliders before building their first airplane.

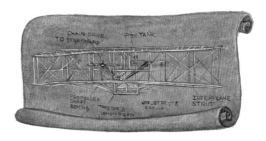

On December 14, 1911, Roald Amundsen, a Norwegian explorer, reached the South Pole with four men and twenty-eight huskies. These men were the first human beings to reach this isolated part of the world.

On December 7, 1941, nearly two hundred Japanese aircraft attacked the United States naval base at Pearl Harbor, Hawaii. The attack left about three thousand people dead or wounded. Three hundred aircraft and much of the U.S. Pacific fleet were destroyed or damaged. The next day, Congress declared war on Japan, and the United States entered World War II. President Franklin D. Roosevelt called December 7, 1941, "a date which will live in infamy."

Birthdays

Many famous people were born in December.

December 8, 1886

Mexican painter of
frescoes and murals.

December 10, 1830

American poet, who
wrote approximately
two thousand poems.

December 11, 1931

Dancer, singer, and the
first actress to win a
Tony, a Grammy, an
Emmy, and an Oscar.

December 16, 1770

Regarded by some as
the greatest orchestral
composer of all time.

Margaret Mead

December 16, 1901

American anthropologist and author of *Coming of Age in Samoa* and *Growing Up in New Guinea*.

Florence Griffith Joyner

December 21, 1959

Better known as FloJo. First American woman to earn four medals at one Olympic Games (1988).

Christopher Carson

December 24, 1809

Better known as Kit Carson. Hunter, trapper, and American frontier scout.

Clara Barton

December 25, 1821

Founder of the American Red Cross.

Louis Pasteur

December 27, 1822

French chemist and biologist who developed the pasteurization process and vaccines for several diseases.

Rudyard Kipling

December 30, 1865

British author of *The Jungle Book*, and winner of the Nobel Prize for literature in 1907.

A December Story

In October 1843, Charles Dickens was worried. His bills were unpaid, his wife was expecting another child, and relatives were asking him for loans.

Dickens was very afraid of being poor. As a child, he had worked six days a week, twelve hours day, attaching labels to pots of boot paste in a warehouse overrun by rats. He would never allow his children to suffer such a fate!

Charles Dickens was a writer, and he needed to write a book that would bring him money. He walked the streets of London struggling to find a good idea. Finally he decided to write a very special Christmas story.

As he wrote, the story began to take on a life of its own. It was full of wonderful characters, blazing Yule logs, music, dancing, roast goose, and plum pudding.

Dickens laughed and cried as he wrote about a small, sick child and a selfish villain who learned to be generous. Dickens decided to design the book himself and make it his gift to the people of England. It would have a red-and-green title page and gold lettering on the cover, and it would cost just five shillings so many people could afford it.

The little book, published just before Christmas, was a great success. On Christmas Eve, the first six thousand copies had already sold out. Charles Dickens had given a gift to millions by sharing the warmth of the season in his story, *A Christmas Carol*.

AUTHOR'S NOTE

This book gives an overview of the month of December in North America. But nature does not follow a strict schedule. The mating and migration of animals, the blooming of plants, and other natural events vary from year to year, or occur earlier or later in different places.

The zodiac sections of this book are included just for fun as part of the folklore of the month and should not be taken as accurate descriptions of any real people.

The December story was adapted from *The Second Greatest Christmas Story Ever Told* by Thomas J. Burnes. (New York: Reader's Digest Association, December 1989.)

Text copyright © 2002 by Ellen Jackson
Illustrations copyright © 2002
  by Robin DeWitt and Pat DeWitt
All rights reserved, including the right of
  reproduction in whole or in part in any form.

Published by Charlesbridge Publishing
85 Main Street, Watertown, MA 02472
(617) 926-0329
www.charlesbridge.com

Illustrations done in watercolor on Arches
  hot-press paper
Display type and text type set in Giovanni
Color separations made by Sung In Printing,
  South Korea
Printed and bound by Sung In Printing,
  South Korea
Production supervision by Brian G. Walker
Designed by Diane M. Earley

Library of Congress
Cataloging-in-Publication Data

Jackson, Ellen B., 1943-
    December/Ellen Jackson; illustrated by
    Robin DeWitt and Pat DeWitt.
      p. cm.—(It happens in the month of)
    ISBN 0-88106-958-2 (hardcover)
    1. December—Folklore. 2. December—
    Juvenile literature. [1. December.] I. DeWitt,
    Pat, ill. II. DeWitt, Robin, ill. III. Title.

    GR930.J332   2002
    398'.33—dc21   2001029243

Printed in South Korea
10 9 8 7 6 5 4 3 2 1